HATSHEPSUT
SPEAK TO ME

HATSHEPSUT

SPEAK TO ME

RUTH WHITMAN

 WAYNE STATE UNIVERSITY PRESS   DETROIT

Library of Congress Cataloging-in-Publication Data
Whitman, Ruth, 1922–
    Hatshepsut, speak to me / Ruth Whitman.
        p.   cm.
    ISBN 0-8143-2379-0 (alk. paper). — ISBN 0-8143-2380-4 (pbk. : alk. paper)
    1. Hatshepsut, Queen of Egypt—Poetry.   2. Women—Poetry.
    I. Title.
    PS3573.H5H3   1992
    811'.54—dc20
                                                                91-42038
                                                                CIP

Designer: Joanne E. Kinney

Cover art and design: Joanne E. Kinney

The lines from "Diving into the Wreck" from THE FACT OF A DOORFRAME, Poems Selected and New, 1950–1984, by Adrienne Rich, are reprinted by permission of the author and W. W. Norton & Company, Inc. Copyright © 1984 by Adrienne Rich. Copyright © 1975, 1978 by W. W. Norton & Company, Inc. Copyright © 1981 by Adrienne Rich.

FOR MY BELOVED
M.S.

Then, my friend, no practice or calling in the life of the city belongs to woman as woman, or to man as man, but the various natures are dispersed among both sexes alike; by nature the woman has a share in all practices.

—Plato, *The Republic*, Book V

For here again, we come to a dilemma. Different though the sexes are, they intermix. In every human being a vacillation from one sex to the other takes place, and often it is only the clothes that keep the male or female likeness, while underneath the sex is the very opposite of what is above . . . for it was this mixture in her of man and woman, one being uppermost and then the other, that often gave her conduct an unexpected turn.

—Virginia Woolf, *Orlando*

This is the place.
And I am here, the mermaid whose dark hair
streams black, the merman in his armored body
We circle silently
about the wreck
we dive into the hold.
I am she: I am he

—Adrienne Rich, "Diving into the Wreck"

CONTENTS

PREFACE

In 1947, when I was in my twenties, I suffered a crisis of gender identity. It was the period after the Second World War, in the forties and fifties, when women were generally regarded as second-class citizens. I felt guilty about my ambition to be a writer and at the same time anxious about my femininity. When I read about King/Queen Hatshepsut, the first and only woman pharaoh in ancient Egypt, I felt I had found a woman who could help me. I began to write about her. But then other events intervened. I married, had children, began to publish.

Thirty-five years later, when the Metropolitan Museum in New York opened its new Egyptian galleries, I walked into a room devoted exclusively to Hatshepsut. Here were her enormous statues, some depicting her as a sphinx, some as a male pharaoh, some as a tender young woman. I felt a powerful connection to my old friend. I knew I had to write about her.

I spent several years reading everything I could about Hatshepsut and her reign in the Eighteenth Dynasty, a period of exceptional achievement in painting, sculpture, and poetry. In 1985, when I was in Jerusalem on a Senior Fulbright Writer-in-Residence fellowship, I traveled by bus to Egypt, where I had my first glimpse of Hatshepsut's landscape and architecture. On the walls of her magnificent temple at Deir el Bahri she tells, in words and pictures, the story of her life. In 1988 I went back for a longer period to steep myself in the haunting atmosphere of ancient Egypt. I found that south of Cairo,

Egypt reverts in many ways to the landscape and customs of four thousand years ago.

Hatshepsut is the fourth woman I have been drawn to write about. The others—the oppressed nineteenth-century rebel, Lizzie Borden; the brave pioneer of 1846, Tamsen Donner; the headstrong Israeli parachutist, Hanna Senesh—have all been intense metaphors for my most basic concerns: refusing to be a victim, learning endurance, learning the skills of survival. In each of these books I have spoken in their voices only. But I wanted to have a dialogue with Hatshepsut. I wanted to juxtapose our two lives across the twenty-five centuries between us and see what parallels might emerge. I wanted to examine her life and tell her about mine.

ACKNOWLEDGMENTS

These poems have appeared in the following publications:

Prairie Schooner:
"Looking for Hatshepsut"
"When I was six"
"Birth"
"Before my father came to the throne"
"I remember my grandmother"
"Politics"

River Styx:
"Nile Dawn"
"Desert"

Sojourner:
"Birthday" ("When my daughter was born")

The Women's Review of Books:
"Hatshepsut, how did you convince the people"
"If Hapi, the god of the Nile"

13th Moon:
"Hatshepsut, my friend"
"Epitaph"
"I followed Hatshepsut"
"Egypt"

ACKNOWLEDGMENTS

I'm grateful for a Fulbright Writer-in-Residence fellowship to Israel which enabled me to visit Egypt, and for two residencies at Yaddo where I worked on this manuscript.

NOTE

Hatshepsut reigned in Egypt during the Eighteenth Dynasty, more than three thousand years ago. Daughter of a pharaoh, Thutmose I, and a royal mother, Ahmose, Hatshepsut felt a special entitlement to the throne, a position traditionally handed down through a royal mother, but usually to a male. At first, according to convention, Hatshepsut married her young brother, Thutmose II, and reigned with him until his early death. He left behind a small son, Thutmose III, born of a slave girl named Isis. Because the child was too young to reign, and also because his mother was not royal, it was possible for Hatshepsut to take on the pharaoh's power. She had two daughters, one by Thutmose II, her brother and first husband, and the other possibly by her beloved architect, Senmut. She was experienced, in her thirties, a gifted and imaginative woman who had advocates and followers among the priests of the temple of Amon.

To reinforce her claim to the throne, she declared that the god Amon, king of all the gods, had impregnated her mother, making her claim to the kingship both royal and religious. In her wall paintings and statues she depicted herself as male, wearing a beard and the kingly double crown of Upper and Lower Egypt, the stiff kingly kilt, and holding the crook and flail. At other times she showed herself as a slender young woman, innately feminine. She refers to herself in the hieroglyphic account of her life as both "he" and "she."

In subsequent centuries, and in fact immediately after her mysterious death, many of her works were destroyed by her

15

nephew, Thutmose III, who succeeded her. Her buildings were defaced, her sculptured face gouged out, and her name erased.

She has suffered neglect by many historians and Egyptologists who think of history as predominantly male. Some leave her entirely out of the registry of pharaohs, or barely mention her name; some describe her as a usurper who was "unable" to wage war or lead men in battle. No one knows exactly what political conflict brought an end to her unprecedented reign of over twenty years.

LOOKING FOR HATSHEPSUT

I climb down a limestone staircase
that ends in a false chamber.
I slide the roof aside,
start to go down a blind passage.

The real passage leads
to another false chamber,
a sliding trap door.
There is a false door

to the true chamber.
An immense stone roof
weighing forty-five tons
is lying on the ground.

It once sealed up her tomb.

Thieves have torn her secrets
out of its belly,
leaving charred bits
of diorite and lapis lazuli
scattered on the stone floor.

But here in a room
carved from a single block
of yellow quartzite, I find
a plaited girdle made of palm leaves,
an alabaster dish
in the shape of a duck,
a small headless sphinx
of black granite

and an empty stone sarcophagus
inscribed with her name:
Hatshepsut.

BEGINNINGS

RUTH:

Hatshepsut, speak to me.

I'm a woman like you,
ambitious, passionate like you.

I often dream of speeding
alone, downhill, without brakes.

When I was six
I drove with my father
in his new gray Buick.

I sat on his lap,
pretending to be driving,
feeling like a queen.

At nine
I wrote my first poem.
I stood in front of my fourth grade,
loving the awe of my classmates,
the praise of my teacher.

At eleven I sold my poem
and bought Untermeyer's book
of American poets.
I read every word, thinking
I want, I want, I want
to be one of them.

HATSHEPSUT:

When I was six
my father Thutmose the First
lifted me up to sit beside him
on his throne of Amon.
He said, Flower of Egypt,
you will be a ruler.

He took me with him on his royal barge
down the Nile to Memphis, to Sakkara,
to Giza, to see my kingdom.

He said to the farmers and nobles
crowding the water steps
This is my goddess daughter Hatshepsut
who will be crowned with the crown
of Upper and Lower Egypt
when she becomes a woman.

I knew that Amon-Re, Lord of Thebes,
King of Karnak, took my father's form
and came down to my mother, Ahmose,
as she slept in the beauty of her palace.
She woke at the fragrance of the god
and rejoiced at the sight of his beauty,
and he went into her and his love
came into her body. And my mother said
How wonderful to see you face to face,
your dew is in all my limbs.

And Amon, Lord of the Two Lands, said to her,
Khnumit-Amon-Hatshepsut is the name of the daughter
I have planted in your body. She shall be king
in this whole land. My soul is hers,
my crown is hers.

BIRTH

Khnum the Potter
father of fathers
mother of mothers
molded my body
out of clay
out of spirit he
made another me
my ka to stay
on earth when I die:
she'll slip away,
unhindered, free,
while ba the bird
wing of my soul
will fly from my tomb
back to the sky

4

BEGINNINGS

Atum, the great He-She,
the breath of chaos
before the world began,
in the brooding emptiness
of waiting space
stirred his hand in Nun,
the primeval waters,
rubbed himself with his fingers
until his seed spurted into his mouth
and out of his body came
air and moisture, Shu and Tefnut,
and out of these came
earth and sky, Geb and Nut.

Atum, the Two in One.

HATSHEPSUT:

Before my father came to the throne
there was chaos in our double kingdom—
from the Great Green Sea on the north
to the land of Nubia on our south.

Men without breasts love war.
They measure their height
by the mountains of severed hands
piled up, cut from their enemies.

But I saw our land laid out in peace:
Thebes, the southern city, the horizon of earth
stretching east to west
and the fecund river cleaving the land
south to north.
Sun and moon
sail from east to west
across the Nile,
from life to death
and back again.

Symmetry. Order.
The Nile
floods, recedes, floods.

And over us stretches Nut,
the goddess who is the sky.
The sun travels by night
through her body,
the moon and stars by day.
Her toes touch the east,
her fingers reach to the west,
she arches over us,
rainbow mother of night and day.

NILE DAWN

A line of palmtrees
against a pink sky
echoes the trees
standing upside down
in the still river

An egret skims its surface,
flies smoothly against
the north-running current:

Tomb paintings
of headless men,
of amputated legs
walk against the current
of Maat, of justice:

Violence and stillness
as the vulture of protection
fans out her lovely wings:

Look: the sun is rolling out of the
sky's vagina: Lady Nut has swallowed
all the stars

7

RUTH:

Hatshepsut,
who were the women before you?
Where did you get your strength?

My grandmother, strong and black-haired,
went out into the world
when most women stayed at home.
She bought and sold land,
made money, educated her three daughters
and sent her son to medical school.

She fell in love with a young tenor
while her husband sat in his wheelchair
designing silver with his delicate hands,
murmuring poetry.

She wore a string of bright red beads
over her breast, she was large and fragrant,
a fullfleshed presence.

I often think of her, feel like her,
feel her power in me,
her round-bosomed sensuality.

HATSHEPSUT:

When I think of the women before me,
I think of Queen Menkara Metakerti,
the builder of the third pyramid.
When her husband was killed,
she invited his enemies to a banquet
in a subterranean chamber.

There were seven kinds of wine,
baskets of fruit, roast goose,
dancing girls with their flutes
and little naked slave girls
who held lotus flowers
before the guests.

The killers were laughing,
winking at each other,
until at a signal from the queen,
a hidden gate was lifted
and the Nile waters rushed in,
drowning the murderers.

RUTH:

At nineteen, I fell in love with my
first mother-in-law,
a New England woman
frustrated in her ambition,
nearer to my nature than my own mother.

I now live in her house by the sea.

Whenever the furnace goes on,
I here her heart beating,
warming me.

She sat in the sun on the porch,
her quick fingers sewing costumes
for daughters and granddaughters.

Her rage to nourish the world
fed every stray.

I see her, a low brown figure
with a cane and a dog,
walking the beach,
inventing schemes for fame, politics, war.
Then she'd go home and bake bread, rolls, pies,
cook turkey, turnips, squash, potatoes
until we could hardly rise from the table.

But now I have lost her:

how she was once young and passionate
and hid her passion under a long brown dress.
How she boasted of sleeping with a moral sword
between herself and her bridegroom.

She kept school in this tiny house, teaching
Shakespeare and manners to each truant and orphan.

She was one of my mothers.

HATSHEPSUT:

I remember my grandmother
Queen Ahmose Nefertari, called God's Wife
and Female Chieftain of Upper and Lower Egypt
who reigned in place of her young son,
Amenhotep I, and founded Deir el Medina,
the village for artists and sculptors
in the Valley of the Kings.

She told me about Queen Sebek Neferura,
called the Horus, Beloved of Re,
the living beloved of Sebek, the crocodile,
Royal Daughter, Lady of the Two Lands.

She built the temple that contained
the labyrinth: twelve courts
with doors opposite each other,
fifteen hundred rooms above ground
and fifteen hundred below,
the tombs of kings and crocodiles.

I even remember my greatgrandmother Aah-hotep
who outlived husband, sons, grandsons.
When she died during the reign
of Thutmose the First, my father,
she was almost one hundred years old.

I remember her coffin, bright blue
with a huge gold cover
painted with a replica of her face.

Her body was covered from neck to feet
by the great folded wings of Isis,
goddess of love, protector.

I was married to my brother Thutmose the Second,
seven years younger than me.
I was twenty-four, he was seventeen.
A sweet boy, but fat and dull.
Not interested in politics,
only in eating and playing checkers.

My father said, This daughter Khnumit-Amon-Hatshepsut,
the loving one, I put in my place.
Listen to her words,
obey her commands.
Whoever adores her, he will live,
but he who speaks evil against her majesty,
he will die.

And so I was named with my names:
The Horus, mighty by his Kas,
the Lord of East and West,
the Good Goddess, the Pious Lady,
the Golden Falcon, divine in her risings,
King of Upper and Lower Egypt,
Ka-Ma-Re, daughter of Re the Sun
Khnumit-Amon-Hatshepsut.

When my father died and joined the gods
my brother sat on the throne by law,
but I, his sister, his divine wife Hatshepsut,
was master of the country.

POLITICS

the labyrinth
beneath the throne
protects the beard
protects the crown
confuses those
who seek my tomb
who want to steal
each precious stone
and chisel out
my secret name

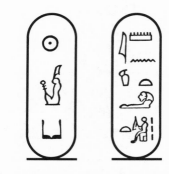

THE TWO IN ONE

RUTH:

Hatshepsut, how did you convince the people
that you were king? Couldn't they see
that you were a woman?

When I was seven
my mother cut my hair
in a short boyish bob:
my hair felt slick,
close to my head.

On the street
in front of the butcher shop
boys and girls surrounded me
pointing and chanting
boy-girl, boy-girl, boy-girl.

What was I?
I had no breasts.
I was I, a lover of words,
not yet male or female.

2

HATSHEPSUT:

If Hapi, the god of the Nile, can have breasts,
I can have a beard.
I live in the perfect justice of opposites:

He bisects the earth north to south:
on each shore lies a strip of fertile green,
beyond each strip yellow desert,
beyond each desert red mountain:

red yellow green blue green yellow red
mountain desert field river field desert mountain
rock sand leaf water leaf sand rock:
power and compassion lie side by side in me,
breast and phallus, milk and seed.

At feasts with my friends, nobles and priests,
and my dear companion Senmut the architect—
in the great cedar and brick palace at Thebes
I wear a transparent clinging skirt
and my jewelled collar of gold and lapus lazuli.

But for the sacred feasts
and the yearly procession of golden Amon
in his cedar boat
from Luxor to Karnak

I wear the stiff kingly skirt,
the elaborate wig with the serpent
on my forehead,
the double crown of Upper and Lower Egypt
and a small straight beard
tied on with linen thread,
as did all the kings before me.

HAPI

In the midst of the waters
there's an island
called Elephantine
from which man-woman Hapi rises.

It is the beginning of the beginning,
the joining of the land,
the primeval hillock of earth,
the throne of the sun.

Two caverns
is the name of the water:
the two breasts of the Nile.
Hapi lies on his bed,
she impregnates the soil
mounting the land as a bull,
spreading her waters every autumn
and bringing forth
from the milk of his breasts
from the seed of her phallus
everything that grows.

Black silt covers the earth
until the crops come,
shimmering green,
sunyellow, yellowgreen
crowned with Nile blue:
sun earth river
reborn in each grass blade
each frond of palm.

4

HATSHEPSUT:

I came to my little brother-bridegroom's body
and savored its girlishness:
plump, white, with delicate fingers and knees.
I didn't care who he was, who I was,
girl-boy, boy-girl,
I loved him as though he were
my mother or sister—
and he—did he see in me
the men he longed for
as he took me from behind?

Senmut, my steward and architect,
born of a humble family,
grew to be my close companion.

He became my twin soul, my hands.

I wrote on the stele at Aswan:
Senmut, the companion greatly beloved
keeper of the palace
keeper of the heart of the queen
making the Lady of Both Lands content
making all things come to pass
for the spirit of her majesty

Still a child
concerned with childish things,
my nephew Thutmose
played war games in the palace garden,
tore branches from the sycamore and acacia trees
for his swords.

Son of Isis the slave
by my dead husband, Thutmose the Second,
how could this child be king in my place?

I said: I will not be a king's ornament.

Thutmose said: I will shoot seven lions
in the space of a minute
and bag twelve wild bulls
in one hour.

I said: I will trade kindly with the Nubians.
I will open the mines of Sinai.

Thutmose said: The foreigners will abandon
their land in fear.
I will hack up their towns and villages
and set them on fire.
I will take their food away,
burn their corn, cut down their fruit trees.

I said: I will make Thebes the horizon on earth,
beautiful with temples and palaces,
the eye of the sun, his heart's throne.

Thutmose said: I will turn their land
into red dust where no foliage
will ever grow again.
I will make mountains of their severed hands.

RUTH:

A bride at nineteen,
I spent the years of my first marriage
in conflict and fury.

I said:
I want to study ancient Greek poetry,
I want to read all the books in Widener Library.

My student husband said:
You must be docile and obedient.
You must earn money so we can eat.
You must type my thesis.

I became pregnant. He cursed,
"That's another nail in my coffin."

But now I knew I wanted books and babies.

In Greece, I let him persuade me
to have an abortion.
Lying on the table,
I suddenly realized
I did not want to part with this child.

I saw myself in the lava mold of a girl
caught in the rain of stone under Pompeii,
stripped of house, breast, throat, eyes,
floating burned and tattered
face down in the eyeless sea.

HATSHEPSUT:

In the birthing room
I kneeled on the warm mudbricks
like any other woman, giving birth
to Meryt-Re. A daughter.

Senmut was beside me
when my second daughter Neferura was born.
He helped me see how I could be
mother, ruler, wife, king.

He was nurse and tutor
to little Neferura who sat,
nestled in his robe,
her head beneath his chin,
while we discussed
how I would build my temple
in the Valley of the Kings,
how raise my obelisks at Karnak,
how prepare for my voyages of discovery.

LULLABY

Senmut, man of peace,
sang to Neferura:

Sleep little daughter
Hathor will bring you
fragrance of clover
garlands of onions
combs of honey

clover to give you
dreams of abundance
onions to guard you
from jackals and deserts
honey to sweeten your tongue
and to soothe you

sleep little daughter
in fragrance of clover
in garlands of onions
in sweetness of honey
sleep safe on my breast

RUTH:

When my daughter was born,
I finally understood why my mother
spent her life pouring love
into her children:

Daughter, turning on the breast of the world,
turning slowly in your vernal equinox,

what can I give you?
War and peace, the condition of your birth?

Feet like seashells, hands like maple leaves,
a white birthday dress strewn with roses?

A seedpod of words? Bach, kisses,
the pleasures of silence? The muscular back of the sea

with its sweet and terrible secrets? You have,
you are all these.

I send you—from the very cave
and core of your beginning—the strength to bear

your peace and war, your music,
your flourishing in the century's despair.

11

HATSHEPSUT:

Do you know the story of Isis, who was
traveling with her small son Horus in the desert?
A mysterious fire broke out all around the baby
sitting alone on the sand.

There was no water anywhere.

Isis, out of the power of her love,
stood over him, legs outspread,
and urinated such a flood
that she quenched the fire and saved her child.

I was not able to save my little princess,
who suddenly sickened with a fever.
Senmut too was helpless and heartbroken.

In the tomb of Princess Neferura
carved out high in the face of a cliff
we placed, along with her necklaces, her tiny cat,
little toy animals carved out of alabaster,
wreaths of sacred persea leaves,
mimosa, and the blue flowers of water lilies.

FUNERAL SONG

Lotus bud,
small and dainty,
I remember your slim arms
as you swayed with the dancing girls,

your eyes laughing
beneath your heavy wig
your child body graceful
under the gauze of your dress:

you danced
with solemn gestures
to the tune of the flute
the lute the oboe the lyre.

Live, my lotus,
open your petals,
let your fragrance fill the air,
dance with garlands in your hair—

do not die,
unopened bud,
do not enter the boat of the sun,
do not cross the horizon.

13

RUTH:

Hatshepsut, I grieve for your pain
and for Senmut's.

It was hard for me
to part with my three children:
the separation at birth,
the flight of each
into the world:

Where once below my navel
I carried a universe, the promise
of an end to grief,
a reason, a surfeit—
now I was hollow,
the beds were empty,
my son and daughters scattered

and I must become myself

HATSHEPSUT:

I said to Senmut:

My heart is balanced
by your heart

take my breast
its gift overflows for you

I'd rather spend
one day in your arms

than a hundred thousand
anywhere else

my love for you
swims through my veins

like salt dissolved in water
like milk mixed with cream

so come quickly to your love
like a stallion on the track

like a falcon swooping
towards its papyrus marsh

HE ANSWERED:

The mouth of my girl is a lotus bud
her breasts are mandrake apples

her arms are vines
her eyes set like berries

her brow a snare of willow
and I am the wild goose

HATSHEPSUT:

My god, my lover,
it is pleasant to go to the river

and bathe in your presence
I shall let you see my perfection

in a garment of royal linen
wet and clinging

When you ask me
I'll enter the water

and come out holding
a red fish

who will be happy
in my fingers

AND HE:

I embrace you
and your arms open wide

I'm like a man in Punt
overcome with incense

I kiss you
your lips open

and I'm drunk
without beer

As Amon lives
I come to you

my loin cloth
slung over my shoulder

THE TWO IN ONE

I long have known
the tender tip between my legs
is a twin of the phallus

an organ of pleasure
when the spasms of love
run from there
to the mouth of the womb
and back again.

My love inside me
touches both my source
and my twin part,
womb and clitoris,
complete.

RUTH:

After two marriages
I found a man, an artist,
who has given me more than twenty-five years
of tenderness, space to grow,
delight:

I said to him:

When your skin is strapped
to my bones, when I breathe
with your breath, wear your small
of the back, smile, eyelashes,
I'll be home again:

but I might cry for your marrow,
parching for your tongue,
and you might still turn away,
so slowly grows our grafting—

until your sex takes mine,
finally, as it was
before the beginning, before
the pregods envied us
and split in two our one

MARRIAGE

Goddess Hathor says to Horus at Edfu:

Here alone in my temple at Dendera
I long for my husband, the living hawk.
It is two weeks since he came downriver
in his cedar boat
to visit me, to make me
once again the house
of his royal temple.

Husband, you need not come this far
if you are busy.
I'll tell my priests
to prepare my gilded boat
and I'll come halfway to meet you

Horus answers Hathor at Dendera:

Wait my love,
until the Nile is higher.
Here at Edfu we measure it
as it rises every day.

I am busy, as you are,
accepting the king's offerings, receiving
the four corners of the universe
to keep against her death.

When the flood crests I will sail downriver
to celebrate our wedding again. I need
to hear your sistrum, your singing.
Horus the sun needs Hathor the sky.

MONUMENTS

RUTH:

Hatshepsut, in the fullness of your strength
you began to create your monuments:

I too create my own kind of monument.

I want to find my own woman's voice, reveal
women's voices in other eras,
women who have transcended the cruelty,
the wars of men.

So I come finally to writing in your voice,
exploring your strength,
your brave assumption of power,
your monuments
marked with tenderness and strength—
your signature.

Hatshepsut, teach me to use my strength without fear.
Teach me to overcome those centuries of docility.

HATSHEPSUT:

Across the river from my palace
in the valley where my ancestors lay
in the shadowy life of the soul,
Senmut and I found the place to set my temple.

The cliffs of rock rose high in a semicircle,
forming a perfect resting place, as though
the mountain held my temple in its arms:

cradled in the belly of the cliff,
my three terraces rose one above the other,
terrace on terrace of white limestone columns,
ivory white courts, the chapels and colonnades
shining like alabaster.

Two rows of sphinxes,
each wearing my likeness;
and on each side
oases of flowerbeds
and hundreds of myrrh trees
filling the courts with their incense.

Here we raised two rows of eleven columns,
some square, some round,
and on the second terrace,
again two rows.

In the north colonnade
my mother gives birth to me
while Khnum the Potter
shapes me and my ka on his wheel
and Bes the dwarf dances his delight.

On the right side of the temple
I built my chapel to Anubis,
Opener of the Way,
who will guide me
through the underworld
to the fields of Amenti.

Black Anubis,
with the body of a greyhound,
the tail of a jackal,
creature of darkness.

4

On the south side, I built my Hathor shrine.
When I was born, Hathor suckled me.

Senmut and I set thirty-two sixteen-sided
columns and square pillars
with Hathor capitals—
her woman's head with cow ears.
The even numbers, the female.

I show myself suckling milk
from the udder of my cow-mother;
with my little husband Thutmose
offering her milk and wine.
Senmut carved his own likeness
in a small alcove in my sanctuary—
kneeling, arms raised in worship.

My father Amon-Re spoke to me
from his sanctum in the temple at Karnak
and commanded me to search out the way to Punt,
to the terraces of myrrh.

On the walls of my temple I showed
how five fine ships sailed northward down the Nile,
were carried across the wadi to the Red Sea,
bringing jewels, gold, weapons
to exchange with the natives of Punt,
who lived in houses built on stilts.

The black queen—enormously fat—
came to greet my ministers; a small donkey
carried her. My scribes and artists
recorded everything they saw.

The natives exclaimed, How did you reach here,
this country unknown to men?
Did you come from heaven,
or did you travel by land or sea?

My ships brought back fragrant wood, resin,
myrrh trees for Amon, ebony and pure ivory,
green gold of Emu, cinnamon wood, incense,
kohl, baboons, monkeys, dogs, skins of the
southern panther and several natives
who were curious to visit us.

My people rushed down to the landing steps
and cheered the ships as they came to shore.
Everyone gasped to see the marvels
as they were unloaded from the ships
under Senmut's watchful eye,
everyone rejoiced to see the fruits of peace.

6

In the fifteenth year of my reign
I began to raise these obelisks to my father Amon.

From the rose granite quarries at Aswan
Senmut brought two long slabs
lashed end to end on the deck
of an enormous barge
towed down the Nile
by thirty oared ships.

My two seamless monuments at Karnak
rise over all other temple buildings.
From any point in Thebes,
looking up, I can see
those huge polished
rose granite shafts
covered entirely with silver-gold electrum,
their glittering tips
quarrying light
straight from the hands of the sun.

RUTH:

Tamsen Donner, who lived a hundred and fifty
years before me, came to me in a dream.
She wanted me to write her life, to restore
her lost journal.

I followed her footsteps from Springfield Illinois
to the California mountains where she perished.
As I traveled, I felt the presence
of the twin oceans on each side of the continent—
the Atlantic, where we both were born, and the Pacific,
the end we both were dreaming toward.

The book fell into three sections:
Prairie, Desert, Mountain.
The structure of a life: early promise,
middle-aged hardship, the final struggle with
mortality. I was witnessing
Tamsen's confrontation with loss and death,
her daily ingenuity in surviving
cold, hunger, cannibalism, in saving
her three children.

At the precise center of the book, on page
thirty-seven, I knew, when I constructed it,
that the Great Divide of the American continent
was the architectural divide of the book,
the line between hope and experience.

8

SAHARA WIND

A hot blast blows in from the western desert
palmtrees bend and thrash

thick sand covers the crops in the field
grit fills our eyes, grit in our teeth

feluccas crash against the eastern shore
flick out of the river like toys
lie shuddering and torn
against the landing steps

the desert attacks, shrouding
the courts and steps of the palace
veiling the temples and obelisks

erasing all our monuments
with tents of sand

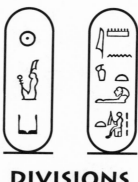

DIVISIONS

HATSHEPSUT:

I began to hear jealous rumors.

My eldest daughter Meryt-Re
whispered to me as she dressed my wig
with perfumed wax and blossoms
that in the worker's cave
above my temple—a cave
carved out of the rock cliff
where the workmen rest and drink beer
in the noonday heat—
someone had scratched a picture
on the wall:

a woman without breasts
wearing the pharaoh's wig,
a clear black triangle
between her legs—
she is bending over
and behind her
a man takes his pleasure.
He is wearing the leather hat
of an Overseer.
They laugh and say it is
Senmut and Hatshepsut.

Others say
that since I wear the royal beard
I also conceal
a three-pronged phallus
to satisfy Senmut.

My nephew Thutmose has outgrown his priesthood.
I had hoped his wish for power
might be deflected—
but now he has become a warrior,
as I feared.

He says:
I will fell my enemies beneath my sandals;
the earth, in its length and breadth,
West and East, will be subject to me.

I will deprive my enemies' nostrils
of the breath of life,
I will take them captive by their hair
I will be as a crocodile to them
I will be as a fierce-eyed lion to them
piling up their corpses in the valleys,
bringing home hundreds of thousands of their dead hands.

I will conquer Palestine, Phoenicia, Syria;
I will capture Kadesh and Megiddo
I will demand tribute of slaves, grain and gold
from Assyria, Babylon, and the Hittites.
I will slay and punish them, trample them
under my feet, tangle the long hair
of my kneeling prisoners around my imperial staff.

I will take back my throne from this arrogant woman,
Hatshepsut.

FESTIVAL

The priests of henna paint my hair
and what my flesh must learn to bear

to keep observers unaware
the crafty paintbrush will apply.

Conceal the wart, conceal the mole,
Disguise the dimness of the eye.

With purple lids to veil my goal,
enameled nails to guard my soul

and perfumed arms to play my role,
what spell can make the great queen cry?

SPELL

spine of hedgehog
ground up fine
claw of dog
hoof of ass
seven dates
set to boil
in a flask
of olive oil

HATSHEPSUT:

Thutmose looked at my temple
with its banners flying,
its hundreds of painted statues,
he looked at my sphinxes, images
of myself as king,
myself as the god Osiris,
my royal beard, my name
inscribed on every marble,
my ka locked inside—

and he shouted to his soldiers
that he was the true pharaoh,
that he would drag my likenesses
out of their sanctuaries,
pound them with hammers,
sear them with fire,
scatter them in a pit,
so that like Osiris
I would be dismembered;

he would gouge out my name
from my sacred inscriptions,
erase my face
so I would be forgotten,
my name torn from the list
of holy kings.

King-Queen, who has seen my face?

Can milk from these breasts, Queen Hathor's gift,
unlock the hate, dissolve the ice?
Can all my kingly power lift
the curse or even name a price
to let me live past flesh and bone?

My enemies now call it base
beardless to hold the kingly place.
None care to see my face.

RUTH:

A young student, I brought my poems
to a professor who taught writing at Harvard.
He said,
"Surely these poems are meant only
for my lady's boudoir."

I believed him:
no one wanted to read about
a woman's life.

Later, when I was pregnant with my third child,
I came to study with a famous poet.
I brought him a poem about birth
in a rhyming imitation of John Donne.

He waved the poem aside, sneering
that it was "musical."

I didn't realize then that he was revolting
against his own music.
But it was clear he was revolted by me,
by my big belly, my female voice.

Later we found him crouched on top of his desk,
babbling and raving.
Nightingale.
Toad.

DESERT

Devouring sand, waiting for whatever wind,
writhing from shape to shape, folding dune
under dune, eating the feet of the granite colossus,
her knees, her huge thighs, her erect kilt,
erasing her waist, her breast, her arms holding
the imperial flail and staff, blotting out
her strong neck, her girlish mouth, sealing
her breathless nostrils, blinding her eyes,
lying curved against her neck, her head,
transforming her mammoth woman form
into hills of silence

ENDINGS

RUTH:

Hatshepsut, my friend,
how can we make a bridge between us?

For you death is a continuation of life:
you will eat the same bread, beer, wine, geese,
celebrate banquets and festivals,
your shawabtis will fish in the river, plow,
gather grapes in the vineyards for you.

For me, death is the end.
I'm racing to leave behind
a few words arranged in a pattern
that will touch the living.

I've seen your Southern City,
the green strips of clover
on each side of the blue river,
the deserts east and west
and beyond the deserts
the mountains.

I've seen your one remaining obelisk at Karnak.
Your nephew did not dare topple it.
He built a wall around the lower half,
but it towers over every other monument,
the highest obelisk ever built in the Black Land.

I've seen your beautiful feminine temple
lying in the lap of the cliff.
Thutmose gouged out your name here and there,
erased your face in places, but left
enough untouched out of fear of the gods
so we know who you are.

I've seen the mudbrick houses of the farmers,
the blindfolded water buffalos turning the water wheels,
the women washing their clothes in the river,

but your palace is missing
and the life you lived there.

We are both women
who have loved men
and other women.
We have recognized the male in ourselves,
the female in our lovers.
We delight in our children.

Standing in the hall of the museum,
when I saw you as pharaoh in your beard and wig,
when I saw you as sphinx with the strength and magic
of that lion-woman,
when I saw you with your royal kilt
stiff before you
as though you hid a phallus beneath it,
and your bull's tail
dangling between your legs
and when I saw you in your likeness
as a delicate girl
with a slightly prominent nose
seated on her throne—
girl and pharaoh side by side—
I recognized myself and you—
the Two in One.

Hatshepsut, how did you come to your end?
What happened to you and Senmut?

Speak to me.

HATSHEPSUT:

In year sixteen of my kingship
soldiers from Thutmose's growing army
invaded the temple at Luxor
and killed my vizier, Hapuseneb,
High Priest of Amon.

I knew this was the beginning of my end,
those clamoring for war
would bring an end to peace,
Seth would kill his brother Osiris once again.

Senmut came to me
begging me to be careful
of everything I ate or drank.

But he himself was the target.
Thutmose invited him to his camp
to discuss new terms
for sharing power with me,
and savagely cut him down.

When they brought his body to me
I felt that my heart
had been hacked out of me,
my arms and legs torn off.

In the Great Place among the cliffs
behind my temple
I had long ago selected a natural cave
for his burial,
high up, out of the reach of thieves.

My workmen dug out the rock
slanting down through the limestone,
down through passageways and corridors
to the first secret room.

On the walls of that chamber
I had painted careful directions
for transporting his body
with its ka and its bird-headed soul

to Amenti, the land in the West.
I was not afraid,
I put him in the care
of Amon, of Hathor, of Isis.

For his earthly body I had prepared
a sarcophagus of red quartzite
like mine, with Isis standing at each end
and the healing eyes of Horus.

I knew his heart would weigh
lighter than the feather of justice,
that he would become a star in the polar night.

4

RUTH:

I came into a room and found my dead husband
sitting against the wall,
looking younger, more boyish,
with smooth unwrinkled skin.

I cried, "I thought you were dead!"
"No," he said, "I'm here."

Full of tears, I said, "Are you going to stay around?"
"Yes," he said, "I'll be around here."

"What are you working on?" I asked him.
"Philip," he said.
"Oh, Philip of Macedon?"
"Yes," he answered, "I've already written
three hundred and eighty pages."

When I went back to look at the place
where he had been sitting,
it was empty.

HATSHEPSUT:

After Senmut's body was split open with a flint,
and the cavity of his body filled
with linen, cinnamon, dried onions,
and perfumed with cedar oil,
he was placed in his sarcophagus.

> May the first son of Horus
> the jar with the human head
> guard his liver
> guard his spleen
> from the Eaters of Blood

> May the second son of Horus
> the baboon-headed one
> preserve his lungs
> preserve his breath
> from the Eater of Shadows

> May the third son of Horus
> the jar with the jackal head
> guard his stomach
> from the Breaker of Bones,
> Breath of Fire

> May the fourth son of Horus
> the falcon-headed
> keep his intestines
> from the Eye of Flame
> the White Tooth
> the Burning Leg

THE BOAT OF THE SKY

The plane has just taken off.

When I see the tiny skyscrapers,
the streets of the city below us,
I am afraid of the smallness
of our lives,
so full of violent
hopes, wishes, connections,
so many dried peas
rattling around
in the tin can of the galaxy.

Riding above the weather,
there is no weather up here,
no whale-streaked ocean,
no bearded heads of wheat,
only a round vacuum of night
with the sun always
on another horizon.

HATSHEPSUT:

Senmut never lay in his tomb.
His body, while it lay in the House of Life,
disappeared.

For six years I continued to reign,
still protected by my priests and retainers,
while Thutmose, growing stronger,
waited.

He boasted of expanding the borders of Egypt
to include the whole world.
The people became greedy for power,
booty, foreign slaves.

One by one my priests, my followers,
fell away. My Senmut was gone.

So when Thutmose, now large and glittering
in his armor, came to visit me
in my solitary bedroom,
I accepted the poisoned cup gracefully.
I knew I had no choice.

I could see that now at the age of sixty
I had done all I could—I was leaving behind
a reign of peace and beauty.

I believed my name and works
would live after me.

CROSSING THE RIVER

desert	meadow	river	meadow	desert
brown	green	blue	green	brown
thirst	bread	wine	bread	thirst
granite	wheat	fish	wheat	granite
heart	mouth	breath	mouth	heart
tomb	lotus	seed	lotus	tomb

HATSHEPSUT:

I passed through the sky,
I walked upon Nut
I came to my mansion in the Field of Rushes
my riches in the Field of Offerings

I crossed the Winding Lake,
the Lake of the Thousand Water Birds,
the Lake of the Jackal, the Lake of the Rushes
and the Lake of Dawn

With my boat of the sun came
nine baboons (who open the doors of the Great Soul)
twelve goddesses (who open the doors of what is in the earth)
nine gods (who worship Re)
twelve goddesses (who lead the Great God)
Twelve fire-spitting serpents

EPITAPH

I wrote on the walls of my tomb:
Proceed in peace, in peace, to the horizon,
to the Field of Reeds, to the World that is Under.

I wrote on the walls of my tomb:
O you who live and exist,
who love life and hate death,
offer to me what is in your hands.
If nothing is in your hands, speak the words
with your mouth (the word can create):

A thousand of bread and beer,
of oxen and geese, of alabaster vessels and linen,
a thousand of all pure things—
and may the wind from the north cool you
with its soft breath.

RUTH:

I watched Hatshepsut walk down the tunnel,
tall and quick.
She didn't look back. She turned a corner
and was gone.

I suddenly felt empty and had to sit down
where I could watch part of a wing
and the tail of her plane through the window.

I thought: now she's in a big steel womb.
May it rock her safely through the sky
and deliver her without pain
to the shore of the peaceful ocean.

Then I went up to the roof of the parking garage
and saw the plane lift from the ground
like a great pterodactyl, nose first,
and climb into the air.

The sky was gray, it was beginning to drizzle,
but I knew she would be lifting above the clouds.

HATSHEPSUT OSIRIS

She sailed past the twelve hours,
led by her protectors,
the Flesh of the Sun, Lady of the Barque,
Maat, goddess of Justice, holding her feather,
Osiris, Sekhmet, the Great Illuminer,
and the Dung Beetle, holding the cocoon of the world
between his legs.

She slipped across the meridian.

Each sliver of dawn
pulled her to the sun.

SISTER PHARAOH

Hatshepsut, old girl, old friend,
man-woman, bearded Pharaoh,
we women too tied on beards
and said we were kings.
We brought lullaby rules of commerce
to the state,
we raised temples and wrote hieroglyphs
and erected obelisks.

Hatshepsut,
you crouch in the silent hall of tombs,
trying to be a riddle.
But I can see through your beard.
Beneath your terrible crown of Upper and Lower Egypt
beneath your archaic stone smile,
your milk has turned to powder,
your breasts are two inches of dust.

14

RUTH:

I followed Hatshepsut
into the western desert
where the circle of the horizon
locked me in its center.

The white disk of the sun
sucked out my moisture, leaving
my body dry and hollow.
No sound. No wind.
My heart rang in my ears.
Space and time vanished:
nothing but frozen distance
inside my skin and outside me.

I lost my history:

three children who had come and gone,
two wrenched from me unborn,
the dead husbands,
my gentle lost mother,
my father, that aged traveler,
even the final harbor,
my last and best beloved,
all stripped from me.

Until I noticed a footprint
inch-deep among the pebbles,
a single footprint following
other footprints back
to the eastern rim of the world.

And I understood:
I had once started a journey
and had not yet reached its end.

EGYPT

A ramp of light is put under your feet
—Book of the Dead

The pyramid from eye to brain
rose up from the primeval brine:

a shaft of light pierced through the dark
and cracked apart its granite heart

Although the hungry thieves of time
intrude upon the hidden tomb

and strip away each faculty
and smash the lintel's final room,

the pyramid from eye to brain
defies the weather of the skull,

insists on perfect symmetry
and baffles the ephemeral

A BRIEF NOTE ABOUT SOURCES

My chief sources have been the Hatshepsut room at the Metropolitan Museum of Art in New York, and, in Egypt, Hatshepsut's own inscriptions on her monuments, especially on her restored temple in the Valley of the Kings. The statue of Senmut holding little Neferura is in the National Museum in Cairo. The following books have been helpful in providing background on ancient Egyptian life and culture:

Aldred, Cyril, *The Egyptians*, Thames and Hudson, revised edition, 1984. An excellent introduction.

Baines, John, and Jaromir Malek, *Atlas of Ancient Egypt*, Facts on File, Inc., 1984. An indispensable book.

Budge, E. A. Wallis, *The Egyptian Book of the Dead*, Dover, 1895. Also indispensable.

Erman, Adolf, *Life in Ancient Egypt*, Dover, 1971 (1894). A classic.

Lichtheim, Miriam, *Ancient Egyptian Literature*, Volume II: *The New Kingdom*, University of California Press, 1976.

Lurker, Manfred, *The Gods and Symbols of Ancient Egypt*, Thames and Hudson, 1980. An illustrated dictionary.

Murnane, William J., *The Penguin Guide to Ancient Egypt*, Penguin, 1984. A complete and authoritative guidebook to Ancient Egypt.

Romer, John, *Ancient Lives: Daily Life in Egypt of the Pharaohs*, Holt, Rinehart, and Winston, 1984. An account of life in Deir el Medina, the tombmakers' village in the Valley of the Kings.

Simpson, William Kelly, ed., *The Literature of Ancient Egypt*, Yale University Press, 1973.

West, John Anthony, *The Traveler's Key to Ancient Egypt: A Guide to the Sacred Places*, Alfred A. Knopf, 1985. An idiosyncratic and highly interesting guidebook.

Wilson, John A., *The Culture of Ancient Egypt*, University of Chicago, 1971. An important interpretation of Egyptian history and culture.